2018 - THE YEAR OF THE ENTREPRENEUR

Small Business Owners – Start your Engines!

How to drive your ideas and experience from city to city with the help of your own pit crew!

Table of Contents

CHAPTER ONE

Why Now?

With a new Tax Plan unfolding in the year 2018, which will encourage Small Businesses to grow and prosper, why settle for a little more profit and a few more employees. This Administration is going to do everything it can to lower unemployment, produce more jobs, and make businesses more profitable.

By lowering the Corporate tax rate to 21%, which is an 18% difference will undoubtedly put more money into research, development, expansion, salaries, and wages.

For example, if a Corporation has a taxable income of One Hundred Million Dollars ($100,000,000), the tax rate dropped 18%. They will have $18,000,000 more to pour back into the economy. They could re-invest most of it back into the company, creating more income for suppliers and vendors, creating more jobs, raising salaries and wages, or investing some of it into other product lines.

ALL of those things put that $18,000,000 back into the economy!

It doesn't get spent by bureaucrats on studies for mating rituals of insects, or paying 1,000% more than

retail for a chair in the conference room. The government wouldn't have that money to waste on programs, that have failed to produce any positive results in each of the last 20 years!

YOU GET MY POINT!

This economy is going to grow both domestically and globally. What we do as a nation, ripples through the world.

If WE can manufacture or create more products. If WE can export to countries that WE have been borrowing money from, to feed our own consumption of goods. If WE have been importing their products, because our Businesses couldn't afford to compete here in the United States. Then WE need to, and will, change the way WE do business.

YOU can be a part of that change!

If you own your small business already, or have dreams of starting one, you will make decisions based on what you HOPE will keep you and your family comfortable, secure, and happy for the rest of your lives. Your family and friends might be encouraging you, and maybe even helping you along the way. But, you are still struggling every day to maintain the status quo.

It is time to be pro-active, and aggressive, in YOUR business endeavors.

Why not GO FOR MORE with the same amount of effort!

Why are you still working for wages subject to whatever this Federal tax plan, or any other tax plan in the future. The government will take the first part of your earnings, and spend a lot of it, on things that you don't think make any sense at all.

Wouldn't YOU like to see more of your money spent on things that YOU could make a difference with?

Wouldn't YOU like to enjoy more time doing things with YOUR family and friends?

YOU be the decision maker!

YOU be in control of your financial life!

YOU be the one who begins a legacy of success for YOUR family, and thousands of others around the world!

That is what ENTREPRENEURS are capable of, but only a few ever do.

CHAPTER TWO

The Race for the Future

I believe that the true Entrepreneur, sees more need, opportunity, and knows more, than He or She can do themselves!

It can't be for just ourselves!

My very first business started, out of a desire to help others!

Yours probably did too!

I was born in 1947, the first Grandchild of a Swedish immigrant, and the son of a World War II, US Navy Veteran.

I was about 7 years old, when my parents moved our family out of an 9-foot by 24-foot mobile home, into a house. It was into a brand-new home in an established neighborhood, in a small town, in Minnesota.

Most of the neighbors were elderly, retired couples, living modestly, on whatever resources they had saved, or were, in some cases, still working for wages somewhere.

I was an energetic, eager to help around the house, kind of kid, with a younger sister and a baby brother.

And I was curious about everything!

Who were all my new neighbors? What were their stories? Where are their families? Where did they come from? How long have they lived here?

So, whenever I had a few minutes, and I saw one of them outside, I would walk over and start a conversation. It might have just been about the weather, as they always wanted to talk about the weather. Or, just about what they were doing.

Fall, in Minnesota is one of the best seasons. An early frost kills all the mosquitoes, and the leaves on the trees are turning from green, into all shades of brown, yellow, red, and orange.

And they are dropping off the trees with every little breeze passing through.

Well, the dropping of leaves, seemed to be a problem for everyone. Because, my Dad and everyone else would rake them off the lawn, into piles, onto the side of the street, which was a dirt road, and burn the leaves to get rid of them.

After I helped my Dad rake our lawn, I took my rake, and walked over to one of the neighbors, and offered to help. He gladly accepted my offer. I continued, working my way down the block, offering to help those elderly gentlemen and ladies rake their lawns.

I didn't ask for anything in return, but always got some cookies and milk, or lemonade. And a few of them reached into their pockets, and gave me a few coins that were way down in there.

The next spring, raking started up again. But this time, those neighbors wanted to pay me to do the whole yard, myself, and asked what I would charge. I would have helped for FREE, but usually, a couple of dollars per yard was my fee.

It seemed as though, every afternoon and evening after school, for a week or so, I had a rake in my hand, and all-day Saturdays. Even the able-bodied men in the neighborhood, hired me to rake their lawns.

THAT WAS MY FIRST BUSINESS!

RAKING LAWNS IN THE FALL AND SPRINGTIME!

If WE want to make a difference, let's help others make a difference too!

Each of us have an opportunity, alone, or with the help of others, to fill a need, which we have recognized.

I am suggesting a few things we can do, to lift others up along the way.

Using the business models outlined in this book, there is room for everyone to get involved.

Let's start by helping a friend grow his or her business while we are building our own.

He or she, might have a business that is not competing with yours. Maybe it is not even in the same industry. It may or may not be struggling. And he or she, may or may not even want your help. But offering what you know, and some skillsets you have acquired, could enhance and reinforce your relationship with your friend.

You could offer to help him or her, do what you are doing for your business, and maybe even, be one of the members of his or her PIT CREW.

How about helping someone start a Non–Profit Organization or Business?

A charitable organization that holds events. Maybe it organizes a large Community Market type of Yard Sale every couple of months, and uses the proceeds for housing renovations, for Elderly homeowners who need a ramp, or a bathroom remodel, or ....

With your initial help and advice, they might expand into other neighboring communities, and rotate their schedules.

A simple idea, and a simple gesture, could trickle down to someone's Grandmother, that you have never met, but is now affected by your actions to fill a need.

How about offering a Non-Profit Organization, a spot in Your Pit Crew? And finance their shares, through your own tax-deductible donation to their Non-Profit Organization. There is a win-win spin!

Sources have told me that the Mormon Church and its members, are the largest shareholders of Coca-Cola. That is some serious money!

How about supporting your local, and perhaps your favorite, Mom and Pop store, by offering them a spot in your Pit Crew?

They might not have the time to go out and spread the word about your business. But they have customers coming to them, who they could spread the word to!

Depending on your type of business, direct or indirect sales could benefit both of you.

Look and listen for opportunities in your area.

Go to Chamber of Commerce meetings. Job Fairs, and Veteran Events, can be an excellent place to meet people with ideas, and dreams of building a better future for themselves and others.

Try to recognize small businesses, with GREAT potential, but no vision! Have a cup of coffee, or buy the owner lunch sometime, and just plant a seed, that could grow into something larger.

Diversify your own business!

When a light bulb pops up, over your head, **PRAY ABOUT IT!**

If it sounds and looks good, give it a shot! A little effort on your part can branch off in another direction, with a whole new avenue of income and rewards.

A whole new (maybe) PIT CREW could be just waiting to start building another CAR!

Maybe that light bulb, was meant for someone else you know.

Someone who is experienced in that type of business.

Invest yourself, as a member of that PIT CREW! You may not have a lot of time to devote, but your business knowledge would be invaluable in that capacity.

Educate the next generation!

Finally, through a Charitable Foundation that you could create along the way, might provide scholarships and endowments, to further the education of young men and women, who you feel can make a POSITIVE difference, in the future of the next generation of ENTREPRENEURS!

CHAPTER THREE

Franchising Your Business

I don't claim to be an expert on Franchising, but I have been involved in a few, and I have bought a couple. They can be complicated and expensive to get into. I learned, as they say, "On the Street". By trial and error. Learning from both, the good and the bad decisions that most of us make in our lives.

I have started quite a few small businesses. Many of them are still running today! It can be fairly easy to start your own business, and make a comfortable living at it. There are a lot of ways to do it, but some ways will be more profitable, and less stressful than others.

I will spend some time in Chapter Seven, in this book, providing detailed information on various forms of Business Entities, talking about pros and cons of each. And a glimpse into how I have set up my own Entities, providing maximum personal liability protection, minimizing taxable income, and in the end, creating NO SELF EMPLOYMENT TAX for myself or family members.

As I combine my Business experience with my Franchise experience, I can envision a simple way for a small business to grow, using a Franchise system.

Here is how YOU can grow your business, or turn YOUR idea into a VERY successful business.

With very little, or maybe no money to invest in your business at all, YOU can get started TODAY!

Continuing with the ROAD RACE analogy!

First you have to form and build a PIT CREW who shares your vision and believes in you.

It all starts with YOUR confidence in YOUR business, being able to grow beyond your current environment.

Can YOUR business not just survive, but flourish, in other parts of the city, state, country, or globally?

The only limits YOUR business has, are the limits YOU put on it YOURSELF!

YOUR PIT CREW can help get YOU on YOUR road! For they are, or will become ENTREPRENEURS themselves!

YOU may already have $50,000 that you will need to start, but you need 9 more crew members on board to get you started, and keep you going.

Depending on YOUR business or idea, you may need MORE start-up Capital, but the way to get started is the same!

The FIRST of the NINE crew members is your spouse, life partner, or best friend. There is no financial commitment from them, just faithful support, and accountability. This might be the most difficult crew member to get on board. Simply because of your relationship with them, and they may need to make some sacrifices of time, with YOU, and away from YOU!

New business ventures, not can be, but are, SCARY for almost anyone.

Take the SCARY part out, by putting your plan on paper!

This is NOT a how to write a business plan book!

This IS a plan!

It is a reasonable plan!

A simple plan!

One that can work for ALMOST any business, on any scale!

The other EIGHT members of your crew, are small investment shareholders, that are willing to participate in the growth and success of the business.

They might be ENTREPRENEURS themselves!

The EIGHT are presented with the opportunity to invest $6,000 in YOUR newly organized, already in place, Limited Liability Company, or LLC.

DO NOT, under ANY circumstances, start this business as a SOLE PROPRIETOR!!!!!!! The taxes in the future will KILL YOU!

Each of the EIGHT, will in turn form their own LLC, for tax purposes and personal liability protection.

Each of them, may also have the ability, if they so desire to participate at a higher level in the future, or use this model as a stepping stone for their own new business. And you should be one of their NINE to create additional residual income for your future.

YOU will own 5% of the LLC, as the General Partner.

YOU will own 50% of the LLC, as a Limited Partner

That total of 55% will give you complete control over YOUR business.

The FIRST of the NINE, which is your spouse, life partner, or best friend, will get 5%, with no financial commitment, just for their support.

The remaining EIGHT, will each get 5%, for their $6,000 investment.

YOU now have $48,000 in working capital to start your business, or expand your present business.

If you have already formed an LLC for your own protection, you might not need to form another business Entity, unless you want another layer of protection. But YOUR Entity should be formed in a state which does not tax Corporations.

Currently, Nevada, Ohio, South Dakota, Texas, Washington, and Wyoming, have NO Corporate State Income Tax.

That second Corporation or LLC, constructed with the proper clauses and documents, when filed, will then manage and control all aspects of YOUR original LLC, and any future business entities created for YOUR business, by any, and all, of your future Franchisees.

At this moment in time, things could not look better for new ventures.

For your Corporation and LLC, the following will apply:

All future Franchises will pay Corporate, a Franchise Fee, and 20% royalties on Gross Income for Franchise Sales, and 2% royalties on net income for product or service sales.

Basic Franchisees will only be able to sell Basic Franchises for a nominal amount.

For example, a Basic Franchise, protecting a small area, let's say a Zip code, sells for $7,000. The Franchisor pays 20% royalty of $1,400 to Corporate and will receive the remaining $5,600 for their effort, in the form of Bonuses on a Quarterly basis. UNEARNED (Passive) INCOME, not subject to Self Employment Tax.

After a Basic Franchisee sells 5 Basic Franchises, that entity can apply to Corporate to become an Area

Director, protecting a larger territory, perhaps 15 Zipcodes, and be able to sell Basic Franchises, paying a 15% Royalty on a Basic Franchise sale. The fee to Corporate, for an Area Franchise would be, let's say $20,000.

The 5 Basic Franchises sold to get there, yielded $7,000 to Corporate, and $28,000 in Bonuses for the Franchisor. Not bad part-time money. Do it full-time and see how much it adds up to.

Similarly, an Area Director, after closing 5 more Area Franchises, and 10 Basic Franchises, can apply to be a Regional Director, whose territory would be a whole State, or one of the 4 territories, in each of California and Texas.

The Regional Director would pay $50,000 to Corporate for the Region, then pay 12.5% to Corporate for Franchise Sales royalties. Five Area Franchises would bring in $60,000 gross, along with 10 Basic Franchises at $70,000, at 12.5%, or $16,250 to Corporate, and $113,750 to keep for themselves. They could easily do that every year.

Becoming the National Director will take a lot more time and effort. Corporate will determine who, and when that time comes.

In the meantime, the Corporation will act as the National Director.

Remember, always invest in every Franchise you sell. It helps to motivate both parties, and rewards you with residual income every time they sell a Franchise, or show profit in their Business.

If you have ever been involved in a business with residual income, such as Insurance, you know how nice it is to have someone else selling product or services, and YOU get a small part of the profits every month, quarterly, or annually.

If you are invested in the stock market. You may own shares of a large corporation, and get dividends every year on your few shares of stock. Imagine how much that would be, if your initial investment was only $6,000 and you owned 5% of all the stock in that Corporation.

This SHOULD always remain a privately-owned business, with only the original members, or their heirs, reaping the financial rewards.

It's a NO BRAINER!

This business model will SUCCEED and continue to grow as long as the ENTREPRENEUR, or the successor, is always looking ahead, setting attainable goals, and meeting or exceeding them.

There are 50 states, with California and Texas, easily broken into 4 Regions each, then add Puerto Rico, The

US Virgin Islands, and Guam for a total of 59 Regions available for Regional Directors.

Within the United States, there are very close to 42,000 Zipcodes. Most of those could be a good candidate for your Franchise. A group of 15 of those could be an opportunity for an Area Director, along with cities with populations up to 500,000. Larger Metropolitans could be subdivided easily into multiple Areas.

If we figure for example that every 7,000 people in the U.S. could use a Franchise, taking years to build, that would be a possible 46,000 Franchises, Nationwide.

At $7,000 per Franchise, means $322,000,000 just in Basic Franchise Sales, would be split between the Franchisors who sold those Basic Franchises.

Can you further imagine, 46,000 Franchises, selling products and/or services, and conservatively netting their owners $200,000 per year? That works out to be $9,200,000,000 total sales income.

That's Right, 9.2 Billion Dollars, PER YEAR, starting out with 11 people, and one vision.

That is just in the United States market!

CHAPTER FOUR

International Expansion

What if, along the way, you expanded Internationally, into Canada, United Kingdom, Latin America, Europe, Asia, Africa, and even Australia.

THINK OUTSIDE THE BOX!

THINK OUTSIDE THE BORDERS!

The United Kingdom and Canada, could easily be done at the same time.

Canada

There are 10 Provinces and 3 Territories in Canada. The Provinces contain the majority of the Population, and will be the most productive for a Franchise expansion. Ontario is actually split into North Ontario, and South Ontario.

So, there is a possibility of developing 11 Regional Franchises in Canada, with plenty of Areas to cover.

The total population in the Provinces is estimated to be around 35,000,000 people.

Using the same criteria of a Franchise for every 7,000 people, that works out to 5,000 Basic Franchises.

Now we are talking about $35,000,000 in Basic Franchise Fees, split between Corporate, and the Franchisors that sell the Franchises.

United Kingdom

The United Kingdom is comprised of England, Scotland, Wales, and Northern Ireland. The Republic of Ireland is not included in the United Kingdom politically, but geographically in on the Island. 5 Regionals are possible there. There are a few smaller islands that are not included, but are dependent upon the U.K.

The estimated population is just over 65,000,000 people.

Using the same criteria, that works out to 9,300 possible Basic Franchises.

That will yield $65,000,000 in Basic Franchise Fees, split between Corporate, and the Franchisors that sell the Franchises.

For easy Math, using these criteria, Franchise Fees work out to be $1 for every person in the population.

Latin-America

South of the U.S. border lies, all of Latin America!

The total population is over 620,000,000 people.

Using the same criteria, that works out to 88,500 possible Basic Franchises.

That could yield $620,000,000 in Basic Franchise Fees, split between Corporate, and the Franchisors that sell the Franchises.

Europe

Europe has 39 countries with populations of 400,000 or more, with an additional 5 countries, whose combined populations are around 200,000.

The estimated total population is over 740,000,000 people and growing.

Again, using the same criteria, that works out to 108,000 Basic Franchises.

Europe could yield $740,000,000 in Basic Franchise Fees. That's right! Almost Three Quarters of a BILLION Dollars, split between Corporate, and the Franchisors selling the Franchises.

Asia

Asia is made up of 50 countries, with absolutely no idea of how many regions might be involved.

However, the population total is estimated to be just short of 1.4 Billion people.

So, using the same criteria, that works out to 200,000 Basic Franchise opportunities.

Asia could yield $1,400,000,000 in Basic Franchise Fees, split between Corporate and the Franchisors that sell those Franchises. NEARLY 1.5 BILLION DOLLARS!

It's a big world, and we aren't done yet!

Africa

Africa as a continent has a huge population, but is so remote and sparse, that other than the 38 Coastal countries, Franchise opportunities would be difficult to find.

The total population of those countries around 1,000,000,000 – One Billion.

Using again, the same criteria, that works out to 143,000 possible Basic Franchise opportunities.

Africa could yield as much as $1,000,000,000 in Basic Franchise Fees, split between Corporate and Franchisors who sell the Franchises.

THAT IS A LOT OF ZEROS!

Australia

Even the relatively small market of Australia, not wanting to be left out, could result in another $25,000,000 from their 25,000,000 people.

JUST ADDING UP TO TOTALS FROM ABOVE, COMES TO $3,850,000,000.

3.85 BILLION DOLLARS DOESN'T MEAN MUCH TO THE FEDERAL GOVERNMENT, BUT IT SURE SOUNDS LIKE A LOT TO ME!

Realistically, nobody could ever Franchise 100% of the World population!

But depending on your business, maybe 40% over decades of sales could bring in 1.6 Billion dollars in just Franchise Fees alone.

Actual product and service revenues, could and should be, more than that amount on an ANNUAL basis!

WHO WOULDN'T WANT A PIECE OF THAT!

CHAPTER FIVE

The Pit Crew

Let's get serious about your Pit Crew!

As I said before, your first member must be your spouse, significant other, or your best friend.

If you can convince that person, that your idea or business can succeed and they agree to help you, the hardest part is behind you.

You have taken away their fear of having to invest money in this venture.

You have taken away their fear, that YOU would be investing more money, which may also be their money.

You have shown them in detail, a plan, which they can see is reasonable, attainable, and worthwhile.

Lastly, you have given them a copy of this book to read from cover to cover, for a very BIG picture of what could be, IF even a little more effort is put forth, by the PIT CREW!

Once that has happened, the two of you need to discuss how to proceed.

Do you contact other family members first? Is your brother-in-law a good fit for this venture? Has your father or mother already subsidized your previous efforts to go out on your own? Have you heard rumblings over the Holidays, that your Aunt or Uncle is tired of their current job, and would like a change?

What about your Son or Daughter? Perhaps you have grown children that trust your judgement enough to get on board, and invest some of THEIR own money in your business.

OR MAYBE, JUST PERHAPS, you want to HELP one of them start a business, and YOU are going along for a smaller piece of the action.

When it comes to family, a lot can go wrong, if even, the smallest, little thing doesn't go right!

Family members as partners, can, occasionally, expect special treatment. The easing of rules or standards which were agreed to in the Partnership Agreement, which you and they signed in the presence of a Notary Public, and are on file, along with the Articles of Incorporation, at your County Clerk's office.

They might expect an automatic promotion to an Area or Region, before they have actually earned it.

Or, JUST THE OPPOSITE! They might have a very good idea of their own, and decide to mimic your plan for their own business.

That would be an opportunity for you to step in and help them as a member of their PIT CREW!

Whatever you do, PRAY ABOUT IT, FIRST!

You might even have picked up more than one member of your CREW already. They might have someone else in mind that might want to participate. Do some brainstorming with whatever members you already have in the PIT.

Your target should be someone who is self-motivated, with good work ethic. He or she should have sufficient time to devote to help your business grow. The real motivation there, is that when they help you, the whole business is elevated, and they have helped themselves.

The members of your PIT CREW should be able to cash into your business. They shouldn't have to get cash advance from their VISA card, which they will have to pay outlandish interest rates on until the card is paid off!

This is a long-term commitment with future rewards. There is no guarantee they will get their initial investment back right away.

Certainly, by the end of the first year, depending on YOUR business, they would hope, and maybe expect to get back all of their investment, and a lot more.

That puts a lot of pressure on you, as the Founder of the business, to do your due diligence up front. And continue to train, and lead the PIT CREW. You should expect them to do their part of the work, as a PIT CREW should, but you are driving the car.

If you hit something, and can't regain control of the car, it is your fault. They might be able to help you put things back together again, but it means the race starts all over!

It happens!

But, you had and have a good business.

You had and have a good plan.

There is no reason to even get close to the wall.

There is no reason to get trapped on the inside.

Get on the Interstate, and stay in the middle lane.

Make good decisions, based on good research and good information.

When the timing is right, use the passing lane to get around a slow-moving vehicle in front of you.

An ENTREPRENEUR can see things, many car lengths ahead of him or her, and makes adjustments accordingly.

And when things are knocking or rattling, the driver gets the PIT CREW involved right away. Together, they get things running smoothly again.

CHAPTER SIX

Everyone in Their Position

Okay!

The PIT CREW is all lined up and ready to work!

They know EVERYTHING there is to know about your business, your products, and your services.

They know who the consumer will be, based on demands for your industry.

They are ready, and willing to help you get started.

Each of them should have a market area in mind already. One that they are familiar with, and have done research ahead of time.

Will your business require a physical building in each market area, or is it a Virtual business?

Can your customers conduct business with you, using only their Smart Phone? Or will they have to drive to your place of business.

The virtual business is pretty easy to start up, but takes time to get traffic flowing.

The "Brick and Mortar" business, costs a lot of money up front, but gets drive by and walk-in traffic right away.

Maybe you have something in between. Like a "Courier" business. You get a call to pick up something, and deliver it somewhere else within a very short period of time. You don't really have a physical building, unless it is just a garage where you keep your Ford Transit.

Maybe your business is similar to one of my businesses in Minnesota. I negotiated a deal with a couple of Sam's Clubs, to deliver anything a customer bought, but would like to have someone else deliver, to his place of business, or home. I would pick up all orders first thing in the morning, deliver them, and repeat the process after lunch. If I even had time for lunch!

The customer would pay me when I arrived with their order and I would unload and get the order inside.

I charged a flat fee, per pallet or container, with rates increasing as the delivery distance increased.

It worked out extremely well, when the Sam's Clubs were filling orders, which were faxed into them by the customer. The customer didn't have to leave their place of business, or home at all!

Unfortunately, I only had one lift-truck, and did all the deliveries myself. I didn't have the money I needed for expansion. And I wasn't looking forward to having a Third Hernia Repair.

I was also spending time in 3 other small businesses I owned.

I sold the truck and the business.

Regardless of what your business is, YOU know what you do, and how to duplicate it.

Now you have the help you need, to take it to any level you set before you!

You certainly, will need to have Agreements, Contracts, and Forms created by Corporate, available to any of your partners or sales teams.

These should be standardized, and the only Documents that are used, both for continuity and legal purposes.

The Franchise part of the business is the key to expansion.

McDonalds and KFC are masters at Franchise Expansion.

A McDonalds Franchise can cost around a MILLION dollars, so it isn't for everyone, and there isn't one in every Zipcode. However, it does seem to be getting there!

Maybe, your business is a service based business, where you perform services at your customers home or business. Such as appliance repair, or home health care!

All you need is transportation and equipment or supplies, and skilled or licensed technicians.

I used a very good plumber who had one truck, and one helper, who did work on all of our "Flip and Rental" homes around the turn of the Millennium.

He continued to work day and night, 6 days a week, until he finally realized that if he had a partner, with another truck, they could not only handle the volume they had, they could respond to even more service calls.

He now has a small fleet of fully equipped trucks. They are professionally wrapped with graphics, lettering, and they all look identical.

He hasn't taken his business outside of San Antonio and the surrounding area, and still runs one of the trucks himself. But he is happy with the level he is at right now!

On the subject of Plumbers, Roto-Rooter is a great example of using Franchise principles to cover every market in the United States, and Canada!

CHAPTER SEVEN

Choosing a Business Entity

These are the most common types of business entities here in the United States. If you are outside of the United States or one of the US territories, you will have to do that research on your own.

Sole Proprietor:

From: Entrepenuer.com

Definition: *A business that legally has no separate existence from its owner. Income and losses are taxed on the individual's personal income tax return.*

The sole proprietorship is the simplest business form under which one can operate a business. The sole proprietorship is not a legal entity. It simply refers to a person who owns the business and is personally responsible for its debts. A sole proprietorship can operate under the name of its owner or it can do business under a fictitious name, such as Nancy's Nail Salon. The fictitious name is simply a trade name--it does not create a legal entity separate from the sole proprietor owner.

The sole proprietorship is a popular business form due to its simplicity, ease of setup, and nominal cost. A sole proprietor need only register his or her name and secure local licenses, and the sole proprietor is ready for business. A distinct disadvantage, however, is that the owner of a sole proprietorship remains personally liable for all the business's debts. So, if a sole proprietor business runs into financial trouble, creditors can bring lawsuits against the business owner. If such suits are successful, the owner will have to pay the business debts with his or her own money.

The owner of a sole proprietorship typically signs contracts in his or her own name, because the sole proprietorship has no separate identity under the law. The sole proprietor owner will typically have customers write checks in the owner's name, even if the business uses a fictitious name. Sole proprietor owners can, and often do, commingle personal and business property and funds, something that partnerships, LLCs and corporations cannot do. Sole proprietorships often have their bank accounts in the name of the owner. Sole proprietors need not observe formalities such as voting and meetings associated with the more complex business forms. Sole proprietorships can bring lawsuits (and can be sued) using the name of the sole proprietor owner. Many businesses begin as sole proprietorships and graduate to more complex business forms as the business develops.

Because a sole proprietorship is indistinguishable from its owner, sole proprietorship taxation is quite simple. The income earned by a sole proprietorship is income earned by its owner. A sole proprietor reports the sole proprietorship income and/or losses and expenses by filling out and filing a Schedule C, along with the standard Form 1040. Your profits and losses are first recorded on a tax form called Schedule C, which is filed along with your 1040. Then the "bottom-line amount" from Schedule C is transferred to your personal tax return. This aspect is attractive because business losses you suffer may offset income earned from other sources.

As a sole proprietor, you must also file a Schedule SE with Form 1040. You use Schedule SE to calculate how much self-employment tax you owe. You need not pay unemployment tax on yourself, although you must pay unemployment tax on any employees of the business. Of course, you won't enjoy unemployment benefits should the business suffer.

Sole proprietors are personally liable for all debts of a sole proprietorship business. Let's examine this more closely because the potential liability can be alarming. Assume that a sole proprietor borrows money to operate but the business loses its major customer, goes out of business, and is unable to repay the loan. The sole proprietor is liable for the amount of the loan, which can potentially consume all her personal assets.

Imagine an even worse scenario: The sole proprietor (or even one her employees) is involved in a business-related accident in which someone is injured or killed. The resulting negligence case can be brought against the sole proprietor owner and against her personal assets, such as her bank account, her retirement accounts, and even her home.

Consider the preceding paragraphs carefully before selecting a sole proprietorship as your business form. Accidents do happen, and businesses go out of business all the time. Any sole proprietorship that suffers such an unfortunate circumstance is likely to quickly become a nightmare for its owner.

If a sole proprietor is wronged by another party, he can bring a lawsuit in his own name. Conversely, if a corporation or LLC is wronged by another party, the entity must bring its claim under the name of the company.

The advantages of a sole proprietorship include:

- Owners can establish a sole proprietorship instantly, easily and inexpensively.
- Sole proprietorships carry little, if any, ongoing formalities.
- A sole proprietor need not pay unemployment tax on himself or herself (although he or she must pay unemployment tax on employees).
- Owners may freely mix business or personal assets.

The disadvantages of a sole proprietorship include:

- Owners are subject to unlimited personal liability for the debts, losses and liabilities of the business.
- Owners cannot raise capital by selling an interest in the business.
- Sole proprietorships rarely survive the death or incapacity of their owners and so do not retain value.

One of the great features of a sole proprietorship is the simplicity of formation. Little more than buying and selling goods or services is needed. In fact, no formal filing or event is required to form a sole proprietorship; it is a status that arises automatically from one's business activity.

Limited Liability Company or LLC

From: Entrepeneur.com

Definition: *A form of business organization with the liability-shield advantages of a corporation and the flexibility and tax pass-through advantages of a partnership.*

Many states allow a business form called the limited liability company (LLC). The LLC arose from business owners' desire to adopt a business structure permitting them to operate like a traditional partnership. Their goal was to distribute income to the partners (who reported it on their individual income tax returns) but also to protect themselves from personal liability for the business's debts, as with the corporate business form. In general, unless the business owner establishes a separate corporation, the owner and partners (if any) assume complete liability for all debts of the business. Under the LLC rules, however, an individual isn't responsible for the firm's debt, provided he or she didn't secure them personally, as with a second mortgage, a personal credit card or by putting personal assets on the line.

The LLC offers a number of advantages over subchapter S corporations. For example, while S corporations can issue only one class of the company stock, LLCs can offer several different classes with different rights. In addition, S corporations are limited to a maximum of 75 individual shareholders (who must be U.S. residents), whereas an unlimited number of individuals, corporations, and partnerships may participate in an LLC.

The LLC also carries significant tax advantages over the limited partnership. For instance, unless the partner in a limited partnership assumes an active role, his or her losses are considered passive losses and cannot be used as tax deductions to offset active income. But if the partner takes an active role in the firm's management, he or she becomes liable for the firm's debt. It's a catch-22 situation. The owners of an LLC, on the other hand, do not assume liability for the business' debt, and any losses the LLC incurs can be used as tax deductions against active income.

However, in exchange for these two considerable benefits, the owners of LLCs must meet the "transferability restriction test," which means the ownership interests in the LLC are not transferable without restriction. This restriction makes the LLC structure unworkable for major corporations. For corporations to attract large sums of capital, their corporate stock must be easily transferable in the stock exchanges. However, this restriction isn't as problematic for smaller companies, where stock ownership transfers take place relatively infrequently.

Since the LLC is a relatively new legal form for businesses, federal and state governments are still looking at ways to tighten regulations concerning them. Unfortunately, some investment promoters use LLCs to evade securities laws. That's why it's imperative to consult with your attorney and CPA before deciding which corporate structure makes sense for your business.

Limited Partnership or LP

From: Entrepeneur.com

Definition: *A business organization that allows limited partners to enjoy limited personal liability while general partners have unlimited personal liability.*

A limited partnership is similar to a general partnership except that it has two classes of partners. The general partner(s) have full management and control of the partnership business but also accept full personal responsibility for partnership liabilities. Limited partners have no personal liability beyond their investment in the partnership interest. Limited partners cannot participate in the general management and daily operations of the partnership business without being considered general partners in the eyes of the law.

The general partner can be either an individual or a corporation. One of the more common limited partnership situations involves a silent partner, where one or more limited partners provide financing for the venture and the general partners run the business. A limited partnership in this case protects the assets of silent partners by limiting their exposure and liability and acts as a conduit to pass current operating profits or losses on to them.

Most jurisdictions require limited partnership agreements to be in writing and, for the most part, contain the same provisions as those in a general partnership agreement-with some complex additions. Legal costs of forming a limited partnership can be even higher than for a corporation because in some states they are governed by securities laws.

Another aspect of limited partnerships is that in some businesses, the limited partner (also called the passive investor) may be subject to special tax liabilities that can offset the tax shelter advantages. The IRS tends to look at these facts on a case-by-case basis.

Limited partnerships file an IRS Form 1065 once a year. Individual limited and general partners include their allocable share of partnership income or loss on their individual income tax returns and pay taxes on that share based on their tax bracket. Partners cannot deduct losses greater than their basis in the partnership, which includes their investment plus any funds loaned to the partnership (except for real estate limited partnerships that are governed by special rules).

The 1986 Tax Reform Act limited the amount of losses a limited partner can deduct on a personal tax return. If the partnership is expected to generate tax losses in its early years, your CPA can help determine whether those losses will benefit you.

S Corporation

From: Entrepeneur.com

Definition: *A special form of corporation that allows the protection of limited liability but direct flow-through of profits and losses.*

The S corporation is often more attractive to small-business owners than a standard (or C) corporation. That's because an S corporation has some appealing tax benefits and still provides business owners with the liability protection of a corporation. With an S corporation, income and losses are passed through to shareholders and included on their individual tax returns. As a result, there's just one level of federal tax to pay.

A corporation must meet certain conditions to be eligible for a subchapter S election. First, the corporation must have no more than 75 shareholders. In calculating the 75-shareholder limit, a husband and wife count as one shareholder. Also, only the following entities may be shareholders: individuals, estates, certain trusts, certain partnerships, tax-exempt charitable organizations, and other S corporations (but only if the other S corporation is the sole shareholder).

In addition, owners of S corporations who don't have inventory can use the cash method of accounting, which is simpler than the accrual method. Under this method, income is taxable when received and expenses are deductible when paid.

S corporations do come with some downsides. For example, S corporations are subject to make of the same requirements corporations must follow, and that means higher legal and tax service costs. They also must file articles of incorporation, hold directors and shareholder's meetings, keep corporate minutes, and allow shareholders to vote on major corporate decisions. The legal and accounting costs of setting up an S corporation are also similar to those for a standard corporation. And S corporations can only issue common stock, which can hamper capital-raising efforts.

A corporation must make the subchapter S election no later than two months and 15 days after the first day of the taxable year to elect. Subchapter S election requires the consent of all shareholders.

The states treat S corporations differently. Some states disregard subchapter S status entirely, offering no tax break at all. Other states honor the federal election automatically. Finally, some states require the filing of a state-specific form to complete subchapter S election. Consult an attorney in your state to determine the rules that apply to your business.

An S corporation may revoke its subchapter S status by either failing to meet the conditions of eligibility for S corporations, or by filing with the IRS no later than two months and 15 days after the first day of the taxable year. Once the revocation becomes effective, the business will be taxed as a corporation.

When it comes to choosing the best structure for a business, many entrepreneurs have trouble making a choice between S corporations and LLCs--that's most likely because they possess similarities: They offer their owners limited liability protection and are both pass-through tax entities. Pass-through taxation allows the income or loss generated by the business to be reflected on the personal income tax return of the owners. This special tax status eliminates any possibility of double taxation for S corporations and LLCs.

That's where the similarities end. The ownership of an S corporation is restricted to no more than 75 shareholders, whereas an LLC can have an unlimited number of members (owners). And while an S corporation can't have non-U.S. citizens as shareholders, an LLC can. In addition, S corporations cannot be owned by C corporations, other S corporations, many trusts, LLCs or partnerships. LLCs are not subject to these restrictions.

LLCs are also more flexible in distributing profits than S corporations, wherein the corporation can only have one class of stock and your percentage of ownership determines the percentage of pass-through income. On the other hand, an LLC can have many different classes of interest, and the percentage of pass-through income is not tied to ownership percentage. The pass-through percentage can be set by agreement of the members in the LLC's operating agreement.

S corporations aren't without their advantages, however. One person can form an S corporation, while in a few states at least two people are required to form an LLC. Existence is perpetual for S corporations. Conversely, LLCs typically have limited life spans.

The stock of S corporations is freely transferable, while the interest (ownership) of LLCs is not. This free transferability of interest means the shareholders of S corporations are able to sell their interest without obtaining the approval of the other shareholders. In contrast, member of LLCs would need the approval of the other members in order to sell their interest. Lastly, S corporations may be advantageous in terms of self-employment taxes in comparison to LLCs.

For more information on the rules that apply to a Subchapter S corporation, talk with your CPA.

C Corporation

From: Entrepeneur.com

Definition: *A form of business operation that declares the business as a separate, legal entity guided by a group of officers known as the board of directors.*

A corporate structure is perhaps the most advantageous way to start a business because the corporation exists as a separate entity. In general, a corporation has all the legal rights of an individual, except for the right to vote and certain other limitations. Corporations are given the right to exist by the state that issues their charter. If you incorporate in one state to take advantage of liberal corporate laws but do business in another state, you'll have to file for "qualification" in the state in which you wish to operate the business. There's usually a fee that must be paid to qualify to do business in a state.

You can incorporate your business by filing articles of incorporation with the appropriate agency in your state. Usually, only one corporation can have any given name in each state. After incorporation, stock is issued to the company's shareholders in exchange for the cash or other assets they transfer to it in return for that stock. Once a year, the shareholders elect the board of directors, who meet to discuss and guide corporate affairs anywhere from once a month to once a year.

Each year, the directors elect officers such as a president, secretary and treasurer to conduct the day-to-day affairs of the corporate business. There also may be additional officers such as vice presidents, if the directors so decide. Along with the articles of incorporation, the directors and shareholders usually adopt corporate bylaws that govern the powers and authority of the directors, officers and shareholders.

Even small, private, professional corporations, such as a legal or dental practice, need to adhere to the principles that govern a corporation. For instance, upon incorporation, common stock needs to be distributed to the shareholders and a board of directors elected. If there's only one person forming the corporation, that person is the sole shareholder of stock in the corporation and can elect himself or herself to the board of directors as well as any other individuals that person deems appropriate.

Corporations, if properly formed, capitalized and operated (including appropriate annual meetings of shareholders and directors) limit the liability of their shareholders. Even if the corporation is not successful or is held liable for damages in a lawsuit, the most a shareholder can lose is his or her investment in the stock. The shareholder's personal assets are not on the line for corporate liabilities.

Corporations file Form 1120 with the IRS and pay their own taxes. Salaries paid to shareholders who are employees of the corporation are deductible. But dividends paid to shareholders aren't deductible and therefore don't reduce the corporation's tax liability. A corporation must end its tax year on December 31 if it derives its income primarily from personal services (such as dental care, legal counseling, business consulting and so on) provided by its shareholders.

If the corporation is small, the shareholders should prepare and sign a shareholders buy-sell agreement. This contract provides that if a shareholder dies or wants to sell his or her stock, it must first be offered to the surviving shareholders. It also may provide for a method to determine the fair price that should be paid for those shares. Such agreements are usually funded with life insurance to purchase the stock of deceased shareholders.

If a corporation is large and sells its shares to many individuals, it may have to register with the Securities and Exchange Commission (SEC) or state regulatory bodies. More common is the corporation with only a few shareholders, which can issue its shares without any such registration under private offering exemptions. For a small corporation, responsibilities of the shareholders can be defined in the corporate minutes, and a shareholder who wants to leave can be accommodated without many legal hassles. Also, until your small corporation has operated successfully for many years, you will most likely still have to accept personal liability for any loans made by banks or other lenders to your corporation.

While some people feel that a corporation enhances the image of a small business, one disadvantage is the potential double taxation: The corporation must pay taxes on its net income, and shareholders must also pay taxes on any dividends received from the corporation. Business owners often increase their own salaries to reduce or wipe out corporate profits and thereby lower the possibility of having those profits taxed twice-once to the corporation and again to the shareholders upon receipt of dividends from the corporation.

Other legal entities you might want to know about:

Will vs. Living Trust: What's Best for You?

by Mary S. Yamin-Garone

You have worked hard for your money and made every attempt to be a conscientious saver. So it's only natural that you want some control over what happens to your assets after your die. Even if you are a person of modest means, you have an estate—and several strategies to choose from to ensure your assets are distributed according to your wishes and in a timely fashion: your **estate plan**. The right strategy depends on your individual circumstances. For some, a living trust can be a useful and practical tool. For others, it may be a waste of time and money. What is a **living trust** anyway? And how does it differ from a **last will**?

What Is a Will?

A will is a written document—signed and witnessed— that indicates how your property will be distributed at the time of your death. It is revocable and subject to amendment at any time during your lifetime. It also allows you to appoint a guardian for your minor children. More about writing a will.

What Is a Living Trust?

A living trust provides lifetime and after-death property management. If you are serving as your own trustee, the trust instrument will provide for a successor upon your death or incapacity. Court intervention is not required. Livings trusts also are used to manage property. If a person is disabled by accident or illness, the successor trustee can manage the trust property. As a result, the expense, publicity, and inconvenience of court-supervised distribution of your estate can be avoided.

If a living trust is properly written and funded you can:

- Avoid probate on your assets
- Plan for the possibility of your own incapacity
- Control what happens to your property after you are gone
- Use it for any size estate; and
- Prevent your financial affairs from becoming a matter of public record

While a trust sounds appealing, there are drawbacks. A living trust is more expensive to set up than a typical will because it must be actively managed after it is created. Most importantly, however, a living trust is useless unless it is funded. A living trust only can control those assets that have been placed into it. If your assets have not been transferred or if you die without funding the trust, the trust will be of no benefit as your estate will still be subject to probate and there may be significant estate tax issues.

Will vs. Living Trust Considerations

There are many positive reasons to establish a trust but do not overlook the fact that it will involve more upfront effort and expense. To determine if you should make the extra effort and invest in the expense of a trust, answer these questions:

Is informal probate an available option? Most states have an expedited or simplified form of probate for estates under a certain dollar threshold (that dollar value varies by state). If your estate could pass under an expedited form of probate, or if you live in a state where probate is not a complex or burdensome process, a will could be appropriate.

Do you have minor children? A trust allows you to establish provisions specifying when a child will be entitled to any assets held in trust.

Do you have children, grandchildren, or other dependents with special needs? In those instances the access or control those heirs have over their inherited property may need to be limited. With a standard will your property can be passed on to those heirs but a will alone does not allow you to exercise much control over their use of the property.

Will your estate be subject to estate taxes? If the value of your estate exceeds the current estate tax threshold, you may wish to consider setting up a trust with tax planning provisions. The estate tax threshold frequently changes, so be sure to check with the IRS to determine whether or not estate tax is a concern for you.

Will you actively manage your estate plan? If not, a living trust may not be a suitable solution. Again, a trust will only be beneficial if assets are transferred into it.

So what is best for you? In many respects, a living trust and a will accomplish similar objectives. A trust, however, allows you to realize other objectives that a will cannot. But those advantages don't come without a price. Whether or not a living trust is better for you than a will depends on whether the additional advantages are worth the cost. When choosing, remember that one size does not fit all. What is right for one person may not be right for everyone. Your estate plan should be prepared in a way that best meets the needs of you and your family.

This article does not address all the intricacies associated with last wills and living trusts. Consulting with a competent attorney can help you make the right decision.

I use a Living Trust for another reason. With very few exceptions, all of my income, comes through one of my

LLCs. The LLCs pass all of the NET income or loss on to one of my Limited Partnerships. The Limited Partnerships pass all of the NET income or loss on to one of my Corporations. The Corporations pass all of the NET income on to either my Living Trust or my wife's Living Trust. The Living Trusts pass all of the NET income on to us personally, as Passive Income, not subject to Self-Employment tax. Lots of layers of filters and protection, and the only one liable for any tax, in that whole process, is my wife and myself.

If you really took the time to read about all of these entities, you realize that each of these have many pros and cons to consider.

In my personal case, I chose not to use sole proprietor as a business form for liability and tax concerns.

My personal situation is not complex, but my business model is. I use a combination of all of these except the S Corporation, as my wife and I have small businesses in Texas, Nevada, and Minnesota

I personally would recommend using a Limited Liability Company (LLC) for any small business of this nature.

If you or your attorney do not know what a charging order is, find an attorney that does. That one section of your corporate documents, could keep you from being sued for any reason what-so-ever!

From nolo.com:

Charging Orders

All states permit personal creditors of an LLC owner to obtain a charging order against the debtor-owner's membership interest. A charging order is an order issued by a court directing an LLC's manager to pay to the debtor-owner's personal creditor any distributions of income or profits that would otherwise be distributed to the debtor-member.

However, in most states, creditors with a charging order only obtain the owner-debtor's "financial rights" and cannot participate in management of the LLC. Thus, the creditor cannot order the LLC to make a distribution subject to its charging order. Very frequently, creditors who obtain charging orders end up with nothing because they can't order the LLC to make any distributions. As a result, they are not a very effective collection tool for creditors.

Example: The collection agency obtains a charging order from a court ordering the Acme LLC to pay to it any distributions of money or property the LLC would ordinarily make to John until the entire $38,000 judgment is paid. However, if there are no distributions, there will be no payments.

The charging order remedy without any right to order distributions is so weak, many creditors don't even try to use it.

In about half the states, the charging order is the exclusive (only) legal remedy personal creditors of LLC members have.

MY OPINION WHY the CHARGING ORDER PROTECTS YOU SO WELL –

Suppose someone files a suit against your LLC, FOR ANY REASON, and the court sides with them, and awards them $200,000. The general partner in the LLC is only liable for his percentage of the award. Let's say the general partner has 5% of the shares. He is only liable for $10,000. But the general partner can legally choose to not pay it, if he doesn't want to.

However, because the suit was awarded to the plaintiff, and the court has notified the IRS of the award as income to the plaintiff and their legal representatives, the IRS will be looking for that income on their income tax returns as if they had actually gotten the money. And they would be legally required to pay that tax as if they had actually gotten it.

The attorneys know this, and in this scenario, will not want to file the suit, and take a chance on owing the IRS taxes on $60,000 or so, that they never received.

My advice – form another LLC to protect your personal assets, such as bank accounts, real estate, jewelry, fine arts, securities, and anything else of value. You don't have to deed them over, just list them in Schedule A of the LLC documents and record them at your county clerk's office. You can revise your Schedule A, any time in the future. You might not need to record it again. Simply get it notarized and keep it in the file with the other originals.

That way you will never be sued personally for any reason.

CHAPTER EIGHT

Summary

YOU searched for **A** book!

YOU bought **THE** book!

YOU read the book!

YOU are, or wish to be, an ENTREPRENEUR!

You have been shown how to fund your start-up!

You have been shown how to model your business!

You have been shown options of growing your business!

You have been shown scenarios, and possibilities!

You have been encouraged to help others!

You have been shown ways to create a legacy!

You have been shown that YOU can make a difference!

You have the capability, attitude, and motivation to be an ENTREPREUR! What are you waiting for!

Your dream can become a reality!

Your reality will change lives!

Need and idea for a business?
I have a few!!!!

Let me help you get to the
end of the race!

You may contact the author at:

rick@ricklundberg.com

Books by the Author:

Available Now:

"Golden Eggs" for Empty Nesters

2018 – The Year of the Entrepreneur

Property-EMall Handbook

Upcoming Books:

The Evolution of Adam – Book I – The Child & The Boy

The Evolution of Adam – Book ii – The Young Man

The Evolution of Adam – Book iii – The Soldier

The Evolution of Adam – Book IV – The Man

The Evolution of Adam – Book V – The Middle-Aged Man

The Evolution of Adam – Book VI – The New Man

The Evolution of Adam – Book VII – The Changed Man

The Evolution of Adam – Book VIII – The Obedient Man

The Evolution of Adam – Book IX – The Reflective Man

Books by the Author's Wife:

Available Now:

Identifying and Healing – The Miracle Series Book I

God Your God – The Miracle Series Book II

Upcoming Books:

Contamination to Transformation – The Miracle Series Book III

www.ingramcontent.com/pod-product-compliance
Lightning Source LLC
Chambersburg PA
CBHW071231220526
45468CB00002B/812